Dún Laoghaire

County Dublin

Map of town

And Surrounding Area
fold-out at back cover

MORRIGAN
Killala, Co. Mayo.
©1997
ISBN 0 907677 98 3

Dún Laoghaire

"The Royal Fort of Laoghaire." 'Dún' is the Irish word meaning 'royal fort'. Laoghaire was a king of Ireland in the fifth century. The town traces its origins back to his time. And beyond. The hills here were sacred to druids. A four thousand year old grave is preserved in the area. 'Holy Wells' still bubble mysteriously . . but now in the midst of modern housing developments. Strange carvings on rocks can be seen . . . their meanings lost in the bustle of the modern town.

The modern town. First settled by monks, fleeing here to the safety of the fort from other areas of the coast which had come under attack from Vikings. A small fishing village grew up called DunLeary. This became the port for the new city of Dublin. Down through the centuries then, each year leaving a new small mark. But not much. Not much changed until the eighteenth century. Then the growth of Dublin's trade and influence combined with the British fear of the French to create the need for a new harbour along this coast. And the new fashion of sea bathing made the area attractive to the gentry. Dún Laoghaire started to expand rapidly.

The first small pier was built in 1767. Imports came through. British warships visited. The nearby coffee-house was a centre of social activity. The Martello Towers were built to protect the coast from the expected invasion of Napoleon. This never came, but the long straight roads built by the military to connect their fortifications became the basis of the streets of the modern town.

The main harbour was started in 1817. It was to take forty years to complete. Thousands of migrant workers poured in, settling with their families on the hillsides around. The railway from Dublin reached the town in 1834. Businessmen and traders from the city started to settle in the new town. New streets were made, elegant terraces and squares built. These were the homes of the well-to-do. The new rising Catholic merchant classes, the Protestant professionals, and the already fading Anglo-Irish gentry.

King George IV visited in 1821. And the name of the town was changed to Kingstown, to remain so until after independence. Queen Victoria visited in 1849 and again in 1900. These monarchs and their titles are still remembered in the major street names of the town. Whilst hidden away in poorer areas republican heroes are commemorated.

Dun Laoghaire has always been thus, looking one way towards Britain, the other towards Ireland. As a major seaport, it is a link between the two nations, a busy crossroads of cultures and peoples. Like all such towns in any part of the world, this gives it a certain life, a certain style. In essence it is neither Irish nor British, neither one thing nor the other. The only certainty is that it is unique and beautiful.

Enjoy your visit!

THE HARBOUR . . .

Designed by the great Scottish engineer Rennie, the harbour was started in 1817. Largely completed by 1842, construction work continued for another 20 years. The East Pier is 3,500 feet long, the West 4,950. And the area of water enclosed is 251 acres. Stone for the pier was taken from Dalkey Hill (48), given free by the landowners. Construction of the harbour cost the then immense amount of £830,000. In 1848, when the London to Holyhead rail line was complete, Dún Laoghaire became the port for the Irish Mail and then the main route for passengers between the two countries. (Mails had been carried in fact through Dún Laoghaire since 1826). The development of the port has continued with the completion of the new ferry and HSS terminal in 1996.

. . . AND THE RAILWAY

The railway connecting Westland Row (now Pearse Station) in Dublin to Dún Laoghaire was started in 1833, the contractor's price for the job being £83,000. (Exclusive of rails, stations and trains!). This, the first railway in Ireland, was originally intended to carry freight from the new harbour to Dublin but, by the time it opened in December 1834 Dublin Port was being improved and the main traffic of the railway became passengers travelling to the growingly fashionable resort of Kingstown, as Dún Laoghaire was then called.

This first part of DúnLaoghaire Guide lists places of interest throughout the town and surroundings. The numbers refer to those shown on the pull-out map at the back of the booklet.

1. BIRD SANCTUARY: Booterstown. This marshy area, cut off from the sea when the railway embankment was built, is now a haven and sanctuary for numerous and sometimes rare species of bird.

2. BOOTERSTOWN ROAD: This is part of the *Slí Cualann*, one of the five great ways of ancient Ireland which radiated out from Tara in Co. Meath, the residence of the high kings. Adjacent Merrion Strand is *Tragh Furbo*, a place famed in Irish mythology as site of battle between warriors and mysterious beings.

3. BLACKROCK CROSS: Main Street, Blackrock. This ancient stone cross with carved stone head is thought by some to be a pagan idol 'christianised' by chopping it into the shape of a cross.

4. GLASLOWER STREAM: Beside Blackrock Church. This stream, which takes its name from the Irish meaning 'stream of the lepers' formed the ancient boundary of the lands of Carrickbrennan (12). A church for lepers was in this vicinity.

5. HOLY WELL: Tobernea Terrace. This is St Nathy's Holy Well, famous as a cure for eye ailments. Attendance at these wells dates back to pre-Christian times and concerns the mysteries of the old religions. Up to comparative recent times people visited them in search of cures.

6. Montpelier Parade: the oldest of the great terraces, built in the 1790's by Molesworth (after

whom the Dublin street of that name is called). Oil lamp holders, the original form of street lighting, may be seen along here.

7. STONE BRIDGE: Brighton Vale. This bridge was made especially strong at the insistence of the military in case of the need to transport artillery across to the Martello Tower.

8. Shops: Monkstown Ring. Traditional (looking) shops, some rebuilt, some original, including the interior panelling of the chemist's.

9. ST MARY'S CHURCH: Monkstown. Designed by noted architect Semple this was opened in 1831 and is a noted example of moorish/gothic. It is the Monkstown Church of Ireland parish church.

10.LONGFORD TERRACE: Original gas lamp standards may be seen along here.

11. ST.ANN'S:1870.

12. MONKSTOWN CASTLE: Carrickbrennan Road. Built around 1250 by the monks of Carrickbrennan, this was originally a much larger structure covering some 5 acres. This and Bulloch Castle (46) were built as protection from the native Irish O'Byrnes and O'Tooles, the original owners of the territory before the arrival of the Anglo-Normans.

13. MONKSTOWN CEMETERY: Carrickbrennan Road. At this most ancient site the Celtic monks founded the church of St Mochanna. The ruins of early churches may be seen here and, also, in the graveyard are the graves of notables. Anglo-Norman Cistercian monks took over here about the 13th century.

14.GLANDORE HOUSE : Monkstown 1857, designed by noted architects Deane & Woodward.

15. TIVOLI ROAD: This is the oldest thoroughfare in the area, forming part of the route between Bulloch and Monkstown Castles in mediaeval times.

16. MANHOLE: Beside 'Fun Factory'. On the right hand side going down the short steep hill between the two roads here the manhole cover is over the original stream. Water may be heard rushing. This stream flowed into the cove which was at the bottom of this hill. The Esso Garage is on the original beachy shoreline. The monks landed here and made their way up this stream to settle at Carrickbrennan.

17. PURTY KITCHEN: Old Dun Leary. Front wall of an old pub, interior rebuilt, an inn has stood here for a very long time.

18. THE DÚN: Crofton Road. Nothing can now be seen of the royal fort (dún)as it was demolished during construction of the railway. The site is occupied by the large office block of BIM (Irish Seafisheries Board) and by Crawford's Garage.

19. DÚN SEAT: DeVesci Gardens. This stone seat, unearthed during excavations, is believed to be a relic of the 5th century Dún of Laoghaire.

20. SMYTH'S PUB: Georges Street. One of Dun Laoghaire's oldest pubs, still surviving original interior in the bar.

21. CONVENT ORATORY: At a former convent site, (now 'Bloomfields' shopping centre, Georges Street.) The interior of this chapel was painted by the noted artist Sister Lynch and is a major example of the Celtic style of decoration.

22. THE ANEMOMETER: East Pier. Installed in 1852, a device for measuring wind speed, invented by Professor Robinson of Dublin's TCD.

23. SAILING BOATS: Dun Laoghaire has several distinctive types of dinghy and yacht, peculiar to itself. The 'Water Wag' dinghy was the world's first one-design class. Dublin Bay Twelve and Fourteen Foot Dinghies may be seen also. Larger boats are the Dublin Bay Seventeens and Twenty-Ones.

24. LS ALBATROSS: This vessel, now the HQ of the Sea Scouts, was a lightship. These engineless hulls were moored at treacherous spots as warning. Their place is now largely taken by automatic buoys.

25. CARLISLE PIER: Built in 1859 for the Mail Steamers. In that era the crossing was made in five hours and forty minutes. In 1860, with new ships, the average crossing time was three hours and thirty seven minutes. In 1887 the last paddle driven cross channel mail steamer, The Ireland, completed the crossing in two hours forty-four minutes on one occasion. The British LMS railway company ran the service with 3,400 ton steamers up to 1949, replacing them then with 5,200 ton motor ships the Hibernia and Cambria. In the 1970's Carlisle Pier was changed to accommodate drive on/off ferries then operated by British Rail and Sealink. Ships now dock at the new (1996) pier and terminal to the north of Carlise Pier.

26. ROYAL IRISH YACHT CLUB: Crofton Road. One of the world's first purpose-built yacht clubs, the building, designed by J. S. Mulvaney, was built in 1850.

27. DUN LAOGHAIRE STATION: This building, now a bistro restaurant, was designed by Mulvaney and built in the 1840's.

28. THE STATION WALL: Built in 1853, this is the only surviving part of the original terminal building. This 'punch finished random ashlar' structure is regarded as one of the finest examples of stonework.

29. THE METALS: Town Hall to Dalkey Hill.

'The Metals' is a pedestrian walkway which starts here and travels several miles to (57). This route was constructed to transport stone down from the quarries to the harbour building works. It was a type of railway, the weight of the laden carts travelling downhill bringing the empties back up to the top. When the actual railway line was constructed later, it followed the route of The Metals. From Dalkey Avenue to the quarry 'The Metals' are called 'The Flags'!

30. TOWN HALL: Marine Road. Built in 1878

at a cost of £16,000, this was designed by architect J. Robinson. A major extension on Crofton Road was completed in 1997 and the complex is now the administrative centre for DunLaoghaire Rathdown County Council. The public entranceway to the buildings on Marine Road was formerly the Post Office (1879), also designed by J. Robinson, responsible also for the spire of St Michael's Church (1892). (The modern post office is in the centre of the town at Georges Street).

31.GEORGE IV OBELISK: Marine Parade.

Erected in commemoration shortly after the visit of the monarch in 1821. The writer Thackeray records that it was 'hideous', but that the combination of balls, cushion and crown seemed apt for the particular king.

32. MARITIME MUSEUM: Haigh Terrace.

This was built as the Mariners Church in 1835 and enlarged in the 1860's. It was built to provide "an Episcopal church, contiguous to the harbour of Kingstown, for the benefit of sailors". The lancet window is copied from the 'Five Sisters' window in York Minster, England. The building now houses The Maritime Museum of Ireland

33. CHRIST THE KING, SCULPTURE:

Haigh Terrace. This powerful sculpture is by the Irish-American Andrew O'Connor. Made in the '30's, it was unacceptable to the religious authorities and remained hidden away until erected in 1963.

34. MORAN PARK HOUSE : Moran Park.
The first ever radio transmitted sports report, concerning yacht-racing, was received here in 1898 from Marconi on a boat out in the bay.

35. MULGRAVE MALL: 1838

36. POWER'S SHOP: Mulgrave Street.
Traditional grocery shop.

37. ROYAL TERRACE: 1860.

38. CLARINDA PARK: 1850.

39.STONEVIEW HOUSE: (front wall is original!) Clarinda Park, 1821. Built by George Smyth, stone contractor to the harbour construction.

40.CROSTHWAITE PARK:1860.

41. SYNGE'S HOUSE: 29 Crosthwaite Park.
Playwright John Millington Synge (1871-1909), author of Playboy of The Western World lived here, and earlier at Glendalough House, Adelaide Road.

42.SEAFRONT CUTTINGS:
The extension of the line from Dun Laoghaire to Dalkey had to almost go underground at the insistence of neighbouring property owners. The cutting was deepened in the 1980's to lower the track so that the electric wires associated with the new DART service could be accommodated under the bridges.

43. PADRAIC COLUM'S COTTAGE:
Eden Road, Glasthule. The poet (1881- 1972) lived

here where his father was stationmaster at nearby Sandycove.

44. MARTELLO TOWERS: Sandycove ('Joyce's Tower') & Seapoint. These were built in 1804 to protect the coastline against the threat of Napoleonic invasion. Approx 30 feet high, towers were formerly armed with rooftop cannons with a range of a mile or so.

45. FORTY FOOT BATHING PLACE: Sandycove Point Traditional 'male only' bathing place with literary associations. The name is believed to derive from a British regiment 'the Fortieth Foot' stationed in the vicinity.

46. BULLOCH CASTLE: Dalkey. *(A separate publication in this series, Guide to Dalkey, gives fuller details of this area)*. This castle dates from the 12th century, built by the Monks of St Mary's Abbey in Dublin to protect the harbour here from marauding natives. About twenty feet up the wall is a sculpture once known in the locality as the 'Dane's Head'. (Rock from this area was used in the construction of the Thames Embankment in London, England).

47. DALKEY CASTLES: Castle Street, Dalkey. The 'Goat Castle' is part of the Town Hall, taking its name from the goat in the coat of arms of the Cheevers family, onetime owners. The castle opposite is 'Archbold's Castle'. There were five other castles in the town, all now gone except these two and that at Bulloch.

48. ST BEGNET'S CHURCH: Castle Street, Dalkey. The original church was founded here in the 6th century, the present structure dating from the 9th century. Early grave slabs are to be seen in the surrounding cemetery.

49 LOTTA, ELSINORE, INNISCORRIG: Coliemore Road. These houses are built on the site where the search for gold by Etty Scott's followers was concentrated.

50 RARC AN ILAN: Coliemore Road, Dalkey. This house, from early nineteenth century, was the first notable one to be given an Irish language name. This occurrence caused surprise and consternation among the gentry at the time, heralding as it did the Gaelic revival and the rise of Irish nationalism.

51. SAILOR'S STATUE: Nerano, Coliemore Road, Dalkey. An eight foot tall statue of a sailor dressed in blue and white. Some 150 years old, this is in 'Roman Cement' and, like the eagles and urns to be seen around Dalkey, was given out by Mr Plasto of Dublin's Brunswick Street as a form of advertisement.

52. HOLY WELL: Dalkey Island. This is St Begnet's Holy Well, reputedly a cure for rheumatism. A Holy Well, also called St Begnet's, is at the back entrance to Quinnsworth's Store in Dalkey town. Another Dalkey Holy Well is on Dalkey Avenue at the railway bridge.

53. DOWLAND'S PLAQUE: Sorrento Park, Dalkey. The poet Dowland was Dalkey-born and an intimate friend of Shakespeare. It has been mooted that the landscape of Dalkey forms the model for Elsinore in 'Hamlet'. The name Shakespeare is a surname still found in Dalkey

54. SORRENTO TERRACE.

55 A HOUSE: near the railway bridge to Ardeevin Road is the house formerly 'Geraldine'. Here in 1834 lived Etty Scott, witch. A beautiful young woman, she dreamed of a vast hoard of hidden gold from Viking days. (Not to be dismissed as this coastline was a staging post for Viking raids into the interior against monasteries and settlements). Etty gathered followers from among the miners then working on the harbour construction and huge (fruitless!) searches for the gold was undertaken.

56. SHAW'S COTTAGE: Torca Road, Dalkey.
The writer George Bernard Shaw (1856-1950) spent some time here as a child.

57. DALKEY QUARRY: A large proportion of Dalkey Hill was quarried away to obtain stone for the building of the harbour. In former times this, and Killiney Hill adjoining, were centres of druidic activity. A large pagan stone structure, named "Clogh Hobber Gillinstone" by a 1768 correspondent, stood here. The 'castle' still remaining is in fact a semaphore tower dating to the 1790's. From this tower signals were sent to ships out in the bay by great wooden arms. Down in the floor of the quarry can be seen marks of cables cut into the rock, these remaining from the quarrying activities.

58. KILLINEY OBELISK: Killiney Hill.
Erected in 1742 by Mapas the landowner as a project to provide work for the then starving tenantry. The nearby wishing stone was built in 1852. (Walk round each level clockwise in succession and then, standing at the top and facing Dalkey Island, make a wish. Which, local tradition assures, will be granted).

59. KILLINEY CHURCH: Marino Avenue West, Killiney Hill Road. This site gives its name to the district of Killiney, in the Irish *Cill Inghena Lénine*, 'church of the daughters of Lenine'. These women lived in the 6th century and the present structure dates from the 11th century.

60. NEOLITHIC TOMB: Shankill to Ballybrack Road. This structure dates back to 2,500 BC approx, making it the area's oldest surviving structure.

This part of the guide details a series of suggested walks in the area. These walks are based on the 'DunLaoghaire Way'...look out for brown and white signposts.

For locations of 'stops' on these walks refer to the individual sketch maps for each walk.

DUNLAOGHAIRE TOWN WALK

STOP 1

Outside the ferry terminal buildings which stand on St Michael's Wharf, formerly Victoria Wharf, this being where that queen landed on her visits to Ireland. Several of the town's finest buildings are located near here. The Brasserie Restaurant is the former offices of the Railway Station. Walk up alongside the station, turn right along by the bus stops. Opposite is the Town Hall, its new extension on your left. Walking along Crofton Road...the building up a laneway between rows of cottages is the former Harbour Commissioner's House (1920). The large buildings next on the left are part of St. Michael's Hospital.

STOP 2

The bridge across the railway. Looking down into the harbour we see two short piers, the landward of these is the original pier before the huge main harbour was built. At this bridge and by the modern office block was the site of the Dún or fort which gave Dun Laoghaire its name. Moving up the road by Crawford's Garage, on the right here were yards where many of the old yachts were built. Take the first turn left and then right into Callaghan's Lane. This area here was one of the 'courts' of very poor housing where cholera raged a hundred years ago.

STOP 3

Smyth's Pub is 'old-world'; equally some of the pubs on the opposite side of the street here have their own indefinable atmosphere. Moving on up Georges Street on the left hand side we come to two interesting buildings.

STOP 4

'The Workmen's Club' was a Victorian philantropic institution founded to better the lot of the less well off. Nowadays, still a club, it is a centre for football and rowing teams and other activities. The Library is one of the nearly 3000 public libraries worldwide funded by the Scottish American Andrew Carnegie.

STOP 5

St. Michael's Hospital (1874) was designed by J.L.Robinson, the noted architect also responsible for the Town Hall, old Post Office, Peoples Park and the spire of St.Michael's Church. The hospital was founded by the Sisters of Mercy and was noted at the time for its advanced design. Opposite here, now Bloomfields Shopping Centre, was the Dominican Convent School. In the nineteenth century without such religious orders as the Sisters of Mercy, the Dominicans and the Christian Brothers in DunLaoghaire there would have been few basic facilities available for the general population.

STOP 6

The Marine Road / Georges Street/ Patrick Street junction is the heart of commercial Dún Laoghaire. St Michael's Church is new, built to replace one burned down, itself a replacement of an earlier structure. The Spire is all that remains of the original. The Shopping Centre (1970's) is either an architectural monstrosity or a place where one can shop in comfort dependent on one's point of view.

DúnLaoghaire walk continued on next page>

DÚNLAOGHAIRE WALK

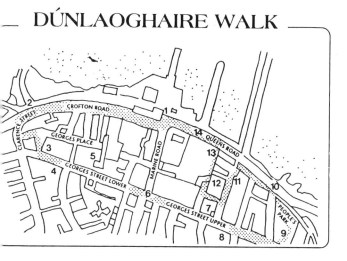

STOP 7

The houses on the left of this part of George's Street with their intact front gardens are a very distinctive part of the town. These are all offices now but at least do remain preserved. The buildings on the opposite side were not so lucky, giving way to two monstrous blocks.

STOP 8

The Kingstown Men's Institute is another of those Victorian concerns, slightly more 'upmarket' than the Workmen's' we saw at the opposite end of the street. A very attractive plaque just inside the door of this very attractive building details its history.To the right off the main road here are many of the town's fine squares and terraces. While many of the houses (and occupants !) are in a certain state of decay, others are being lovingly restored. Worth a brief detour off the Way. In pre Dún Laoghaire days this particular area was called Kilahulshone, a name implying the presence of an early-Christian setttement.

STOP 9

The People's Park is on the site of a quarry. A formal Victorian Park, it is very attractive. Note the fine restored fountains and the modern 'blind garden', this layout of plants can be identified by their scent and by the braille signs alongside.

STOP 10

Sea Baths.

STOP 11.

The statue of Christ the King is by the American-Irish sculptor Andrew O'Connor, (1874-1941).Actually intended as a memorial to the dead of the First World War, for many years it lay in a   back garden, hidden, having displeased the religious authorities. Tastes and understanding change and now it stands here, a powerful and compelling work.

STOP 12.

Maritime Museum.

STOP 13

Moran Park House was a residence for the Harbour Master. The grounds are now a public park. The water filled quarry was used as a reservoir

*DúnLaoghaire Walk continued from facing page

for watering ships - a pipe ran from here to the pier. This house was site of 'world's first sports broadcast', the (half-Irish) Marconi sending in a yacht race report by radio from out in the bay.

STOP 14

Moving back out on to the 'Metals', walk to the left towards the elaborate seafront gates of the Marine Hotel. Turn right here and cross the road to the 'George IV Obelisk', (1821). Out on the viewing platform here you will note the memorial stone to the lifeboatmen. The pier below is the Carlisle Pier; originally the railway ran right down this to meet the 'Mail Boat', now called 'Car Ferry'. The building below to the right is the National Yacht Club (1870), that to the left The Royal St.George Yacht Club (1843). The names of these clubs tell of their different social and political origins; nowadays the membership is fairly indistInguishable. Proceed from here along the elegant Marine Parade towards the station and the end of this walk.

BLACKROCK WALK

Originally Newtown Castle Byrne, the present name for the town derives from a black rock that used to be obvious off the shore. This rock was the eastern boundary of Dublin's city limits.

*Blackrock Walk numbers are on map on page 19

STOP 1

Blackrock DART station. The public baths on the sea side of the line were built in 1834, washed away in 1886 and re-built, and now lie closed pending bureaucratic decisions. (Which could take some time!). Note the memorial to Barney Heron, one of Ireland's great divers, on the wall beside the pedestrian footbridge. Proceed from here along Idrone Terrace (1870). Note pediment in centre, Idrone Sur Mer.

STOP 2

Just before we turn inland we can have a peer over the wall here. The little harbour is named after one Thomas Vance. The classical pavilion was for the enjoyment of Lord Cloncurry who owned the land around here; the elaborate foot-bridge was built at his insistence in return for allowing the railway to pass through his grounds. Proceeding up towards the main road, note Idrone Lane on the left and, among the mews the remains of an elaborate stables. At the main road, turn left.

STOP 3.

Newtown Avenue has nothing really to do with 'new', the word being a corruption of the personal name Naoi an early-Irish character of unknown sex or occupation who also gives his/her name to Tobernea, 'The Well of Naoi', a Holy Well on the shoreline up ahead. (Not on this walk, but the interested should proceed to Tobernea Terrace climb down a cliff, across a games pitch, and up another cliff. (The water is noted as a cure for the eyes).

STOP 4

Blackrock House still stands, on the left. Built in 1774 by an English rogue called John Lees, Secretary of The Post Office. This job was a sort of family fiefdom for his family, himself and son Sir Harcourt Lees being noted for the scale of their embezzlement. Nice house though, and the scene of great partying by the gentry (which means, then as now, all the other rogues in Dublin) in the 18th and early 19th centurys. Behind the house may be seen a Trachycarpus Excelsa (a real palm tree) growing beside a Cordylina Australis (so-called palm tree).

STOP 5

Opposite Blackrock House can be seen a car showrooms which was the tramyard. The small houses alongside, now called Newtown Villas, were once called Tram Cottages, being built by the company for its employees.

STOP 6

Moving up towards the hill ahead. (The Holy Well is off to our left). The small park on the left is riddled with underground bunkers, built as air raid shelters in the second world war. The red thing is a sculpture.

BLACKROCK WALK

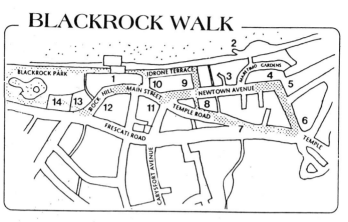

STOP 7

Down the Blackrock By-pass, opened in recent years in the foolish hope that it would solve the traffic problems. There's a church buried somewhere under this road. But a church is nothing to an Irish road engineer! Cathedrals, houses, streets, whole neighbourhoods are threatened and often swept away. Also buried under this road is the Glas Lobhar River, in English known as the Leper's Stream. It runs down from a locality, Leopardstown, where there used be a leper colony. The river/stream formed the ancient boundary between Monkstown and Thorncastle, the latter another early name for Blackrock.

STOP 8

The Church of St. John The Baptist is a very fine Irish Gothic job, designed by Pugin and Byrne. It contains a window by the noted stained glass artist Evie Hone.

STOP 9

Move down the alleyway to the left, this known by old locals 'Charlie Chucks'. At one time it was lined with cottages. Small cottages. The Glas Lobhar stream can be seen on the other side of the church.

STOP 10

In Newtown Avenue again, though its real name is Byrnes Road. The Town Hall dates from 1865, the Library from 1904. The Methodist Church dates from 1861 (when it cost £1250 to build). The Blackrock Cross dates from no-one really knows, but is likely to be at least 1000 years old. It has been moved in recent times, and now faces the opposite direction than it did for those 1000 years. (Road engineers!). At one time it was a point on the city boundary, and a place for funerals to congregate, though it is felt this latter had more to do with the nearby 18th century Three Tun pub, now gone.

STOP 11

On the left of Main Street there lies hidden another line of houses, the 18th century houses now used by Blackrock Market. At the corner of Georges Avenue (opposite the bookies) there used be Conways Tavern, the Annual Melon Feast was held here in the 18th century. They knew how to have a good time in those days.

STOP 12

Blackrock Shopping Centre is fashionable. This is the place to be seen buying your groceries.

STOP 13

Ahead, the Rock Road is part of Slighe Cualann, one of the ancient roads leading to Tara. At the gates of Blackrock Park was another large house called Elmcliff. Now vanished, it was later a sort of upmarket 18th century knocking shop, and is not to be confused with Lios an Uisce, the surviving large house associated with John Wesley, who visited in 1775. This was residence of a Lady Denny, granddaughter of the nasty bit of Cromwellian work, Sir William Petty. But Lady Arabella was a decent old skin (local expression) who did good works and tried to introduce silk worms to Ireland.

STOP 14

The park is attractive, built in the 1880's to replace the noisome swamps left after the railway cut off the area from the sea. A laneway at the railway side of the park leads directly into the DART station.

MONKSTOWN WALK

Monkstown takes its English-language name from the monks who for many centuries owned and farmed the lands around here. The older irish-language name lies hidden in the word 'Carrickbrennan', likely to derive from The Rock of Broen', this Broen being an 11th century ruler.

STOP 1

Monkstown Ring, surrounded by a cut stone wall. Note central 'palm tree', actually Cordylina Australis; these sub-tropical trees grow well in this district. The flower planter is a disused horse trough. Monkstown Village is noted for traditional shopfronts and its two fine churches. Before moving on it is worth taking a short detour up the public avenue marked 'Cheshire Home'. Not far up here we see a stream coming along the centre of the valley. Along this and other streams the early monks made their way up from the shore.

STOP 2

Back at the main road, the church (Church of Ireland) is a distinctive Moorish-Gothic edifice (designed by John Semple, c 1830) built around the fabric of an earlier church. Alongside is the 1791 Primary School; only closed in recent years.

STOP 3

St Patrick's (Roman Catholic) Church is a very fine 'Irish Gothic' building (design Puginl/Ashlin 1861). Continue along Carrickbrennan Road- the corner of Pakenham Road is the Friends' (Quaker) Meeting House. Names such as Pakenham and De Vesci in this area derive from the former Anglo-Irish landowning families. Carrickbrennan Road has been widened in recent years, the stone walls re-built along both sides.

STOP 4

Carrickbrennan Graveyard contains many interesting graves and, tended by a local historical society, is a tranquil and thoughtful spot. Celtic monks are believed to have come here in the 9th century, fleeing, it is said, from areas more vulnerable to Viking attack. Their church, of St. Mochanna, is gone; the present ruins date from the 17th century. The Celtic monks had been more or less thrown out after the Norman Invasion by the Anglo-Norman Cistercians of St Mary's in Dublin. The Cistercians in turn gave way to a   Protestant congregation after the Reformation.

STOP 5

The remains of Monkstown Castle are still reasonably impressive but bear little relationship to the onetime size and importance of this site. Originally built by the Cistercians (of St.Mary's Abbey, Dublin) to protect their lands, after the dissolution of the monasteries it passed into the hands of a succession of generals, thugs, place seekers, mercenaries. . . and a protestant bishop.The Pakenhams (the english Lord Longford and his writer daughter Lady Antonia Fraser) are descended from this bishop. A onetime occupant here was General Ludlow, one of the 'regicides' responsible for the execution of Charles the First of England.

STOP 6

Move now up 'Widow Gamble's Hill' to the left at the roundabout. Note the walls along the right hand side and the unusual number of square cut stones in the rubble. These are remnants of the castle buildings.   St John's Church, at the York Road Crossroads, is a former Church of Ireland (Anglican Communion) building, now used by Roman Catholic 'Tridentines', (Latin Mass Rite).Tivoli Road opposite is   the   most   ancient   thoroughfare   in   the neighbourhood, being part of the route between Dublin City and the harbour at Dalkey. Another horse trough behind ring of trees.

STOP 7

Knapton Road is what is known in Dublin as 'a relic of old decency'; quiet, secluded, and comfortable.   Note   the   attractive   Victorian architecture, the use of stone, brick and iron in the houses, and the granite kerbstones on the right hand footpath.   These   kerbs   signify   the   original DunLaoghaire streets. The end house, 'Knapton', is a centre for the Opus Dei religious movement. The hollow at Vesey Place is a former old quarry, now for many years a park. Note the remains of an old gas light column on your right.

MONKSTOWN WALK

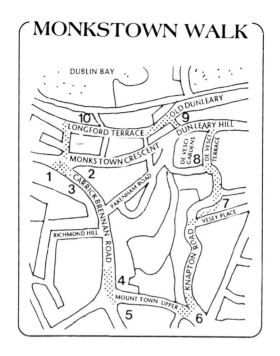

STOP 8

De Vesci Gardens, not a public park, contains the 'Dún Seat'; a strange throne-like stone chair allegedly dug up from the ancient remains of Laoghaire's Dún. The bizarre twosome on De Vesci Terrace are Castor and Pollux. They stand on each side of the De Vesci family coat of arms. Back at the main road, turn left and down the hill. Note the original height of the wall on your right hand; look through the section of railing. This cliff leads to the onetime edge of the water, now filled in and covered in apartments.

STOP 9

The steep hill by the children's entertainment institution, onetime ballroom of romance, leads to Old Dunleary, the remains of the gruesome waterfront village which existed before the construction of the harbour. (Pause halfway down; that water- rushing sound is the same stream, now underground, you saw behind Monkstown

Village).The bottom of this hill was the beach. The petrol station is the site of the 'Coffee House', a watering place for the gentry in the 18th century. Proceed to your left at the bottom of the hill. There were originally small houses on both sides of this roadway, noted for squalor and overcrowding. All has changed. On the right, now modern apartments, was the famous Salthill Hotel. This 'Salt Hill' takes its name from onetime salt pans on the shoreline beyond, now - covered by a sewage pumping station. Next on the right, these entrance columns to the apartment complex were salvaged from a disused rural church. There are a lot of disused churches in modern Ireland. Above on the left hand side is Longford Terrace, one of the great planned terraces of the onetime 'Kingstown'. This is great stuff, architecturally speaking. In decline up to recent years, the houses in this terrace were generally broken up into rooms and flats, occupied by a mix of decayed gentry and artistic riff-raff of various persuasions. Now the terrace is changing again, moving back into single family occupation. A house here can cost a quarter of a million pounds.

STOP 10

This land between road and railway was formerly the gardens of the fine houses on the left hand side of the road, the road itself being actually 'private'. All this has passed into memory. Right by the station in 1807 two troopships were dashed up on the rocks in a storm, leading to the deaths of over 400 people. Their bodies lie in all the little graveyards along this coast. Disasters like this led to the building of the harbour. Though long after the harbour was built the civilian ship Leinster was torpedoed in the First World War and went down out in the bay. Hundreds of bodies were washed up right here. They too lie in little graveyards along the coast. Something sad and strange about this shore. Always has been. In one of the ancient stories of Ireland a warrior walked here. He fought with the sea birds. They turned into warriors themselves and drove him away. Naked, he walked on to Tara, the capital of the country. And there they made him king.

KILLINEY WALK

A placename formed from the anglicised sound of the Irish-language Cill Inghena Lenine, meaning 'Church of the Daughters of Lenine'

STOP 1.

The greater part of Killiney Village lies up the lanes and small roads behind the Druids Chair Pub, a flavour of the place can be gained by wandering up here. The view to your south is the Vale of Shanganagh, the first of the Wicklow Mountains forming a backdrop. Proceed down hill, your back to the view, in a northerly direction. At the entrance to the Rock lodge houses the view is over the whole city of Dublin. Proceed a further short distance, the entrance to Killiney Hill Park is on the right.

STOP 2.

The plates on the entrance pillars relate the history of this park. (Before entering you might detour slightly downhill to two small attractive churches, one modern, one old, one Roman Catholic, one Church of Ireland, on opposite sides of the road, naturally!) Inside the park gates the small tower is the remains of the entrance lodge. The sculpture is the remains of two tons of bronze. Proceed upwards to the right.

STOP 3

At the halfway stage the path flattens out. The grassy hump on the right is a water reservoir. The flight of steps leads back down to the village. From here on up the view starts to speak for itself. The DART line may be seen creeping round the edge of the bay. The town in the distance is BRAY under the great mass of Bray Head. The hill in the middle distance is Cathygollagher, note the old lead mine ventilation tower. The high volcanic looking (but not of volcanic origin mountain beyond is the Sugarloaf.

STOP 4

The Obelisk was built in 1742 by a John Mapas the hills walled in as a deerpark at around the same time. The oft-stated reason for their construction was 'to provide work for the poor'- these 'poor' being the landless native Irish displaced by the system under which John Mapas prospered.

prospered!) However, the view here being more agreeable than the facts of history we'll continue looking around. From here it is sometimes possible to see the mountains of Wales, mirage-like, on the far horizon. Below us is Dalkey Island. The structure on the east is an old defensive battery. (The British were very keen to 'defend' this area from outsiders, not apparently noticing that the enemy lay within!). The Martello tower in the centre is positioned to be in view of others along the coast, to the north and the south, these being built to form a continuous chain of sight back to Dublin Castle. The other structure on the island is St Begnet's Church, a Celtic religious foundation This church was built from the stones of the 'Dún (fort) of Sedgha'. Sedgha was a Milesian ruler in 17OObc. These Milesians were of Spanish origin. Strangely, the church was apparently built 2000 years after Sedgha by more Spaniards, the unit of measurement used in its construction being the Vara, or 'Castilian Yard'. Looking northwards, we see Dún Laoghaire below and can appreciate the size of the enormous artificial harbour. Along the coast is Merrion Strand taking its name from the old Irish meaning 'white sea'. Across the bay the peninsula of Howth. The city of Dublin stretches out in all directions. Right beside us on the hill is The Wishing Stone of 1852. This is actually a memorial to a man killed in a hunting accident but is now used to make wishes or get good luck. People walk around it in a clockwise direction on each level; at the top one makes the wish. This is a reflection of a most ancient pagan custom; in the west of Ireland to this day people walk clockwise around 'stations', (usually prehistoric remains) as part of pilgrimages. Women wishing to acquire the power of witchcraft walked (naked) in an anti-clockwise direction. But visitors should not do this on Killiney Hill!) Doubtless, long before the wishing stone, the hill was used for all these rituals, people walking round some long vanished prehistoric structure. The remains of this (a bronze age passage grave?) may very well lie under John Mapas' obelisk. The little baby obelisk was a trial

Killiney Walk continued on following page >

model for the first. But proceeding onwards we will move down through the woods, heading for Dalkey Hill which we can see from here across the tree tops. Take the path on the right hand side leading into the woods. Follow this path down through the woods...the concrete tables were constructed for the convenience of picnic parties. ..and at the bottom take the path up alongside the woods to the top of Dalkey Hill.

STOP 5

The radio beacon is used for aircraft navigation. Interestingly a similar route is used by migrating birds as the aircraft which come in to Dublin Bay over here. Peer over the wall at the quarry face. Sometimes climbing clubs may be seen practicing here. These quarries were, of course, opened up to provide stone for the construction of the piers which you may see beyond. The 'Castle', so-called, is actually a signalling tower. This was used to send messages by semaphore to ships out in the bay in the anxious times of the Napoleonic Wars. Move down the hill, along the narrow winding path, keeping the quarry wall to our right. At the bottom of this right-of-way we turn left, finding ourselves at Torca Road and Shaw's Cottage is up to our left.

Killiney Walk continued on following page >

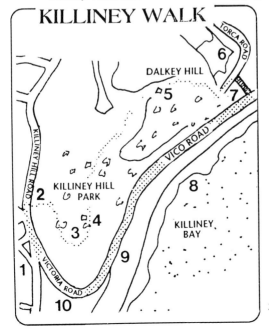

STOP 6

The 'Cat's Ladder', easier to descend than other- wise, leads us down onto Vico Road. At the bottom we turn right and, crossing the road, take one of the little paths leading down on to the beach. On the cliffs may be seen the Cineroria Jocobaea, a hybrid of the Mediterranean Seneclo Cineraria and the local ragwort.

STOP 7

Nice View.

STOP 8.

Whiterock Beach. Formerly very popular, not so these days, perhaps because people can't bring motor cars down the steps. Whiterock was the scene of a mine in the 1700's. Among the cliff face may be seen one of the shafts; this latterly became known to locals as Deco's Cave, after an eccentric vagrant chartacter who lived in there, sleeping in a hammock. Now gone, as they say, to his maker.

STOP 9

Mount Eag!e was built in the mid 1900's by one Robert Warren, then owner of most of the locality. The house is built, unusual for this area, of cut stone and is said to have beautiful gardens. Which are private. Warren's name can still be made out on plaques on the various structures around the hills; the Obelisk, the 'Castle' on Dalkey Hill, and the gate lodge at the park entrance. Warren lived in the house which now forms the core of Fitzpatrick's Castle Hotel. His name is on a plaque there too. False modesty does not seem to have been one of his failings.

STOP 10

Ayesha Castle, although a private residence, is open to the public on certain days. Also a Warren family house, the road we are now on was formerly its private avenue, leading down from that entrance arch at Killiney Village. This is our destination, and the end of the walk.

SANDYCOVE WALK

The origins of the placename are obvious, this once being a sandy Inlet on an otherwise bleakly rocky and inhospitable coastline. The Irish-language name is Cuas an Gainmh.

Sandycove Walk map is on following page.

STOP 1

The DART Station. Turn right coming out, cross the road and proceed down Islington Avenue. This mix of Edwardian and Victorian architecture, is typical of a seaside town of the period.

STOP 2

Note the fine terraced houses and on the right are smaller seaside villas. Further down on left the arched gateway is to what once were the mews houses of the large terrace on the seafrount. These mews, once the homes of horses and domestic menials, are now in cases considered more desirable than residences to which they belonged.

STOP 3

Cross the road at the bottom and proceed onto the promenade. This is all reclaimed land, the top of the old sea wall with rounded granite stone may be seen protruding onto the footpath. This short length of wall is all that remains of the sea wall in L.A.G.Strong's noted (and very peculiar) book, 'Sea Wall'. Strong lived at what is now a car sales lot beside the Forum Cinema.

STOP 4

Out on the 'new' sea wall, built in the 1950's. From left to right the view takes in Dún Laoghaire's East Pier, on the opposite side of Dublin Bay the peninsula of Howth, in Irish *Ben Eadair*. Those larger buoys and markers are for yacht races, the smaller for lobster fishermen. This Scotsman's Bay, now a haunt of pleasure craft and windsurfers. However, before the construction of the harbour, this pleasant bay was a noted graveyard for ships which were driven onto the rocky coast. The large black birds standing on these rocks are cormorants.

Sandycove Walk continued on following page >

SANDYCOVE WALK

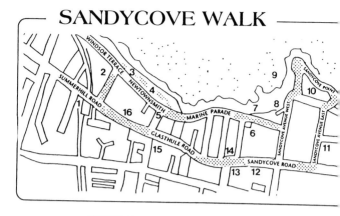

STOP 5

Back on the road at a structure commemorating the 1921-22 construction of the road along here, Marine Parade. Opposite is Link Road, and, to the right of that, an area known as Newtownsmith. Proceed along the road towards the Tower. An attractive band of houses on the landward side with their interesting names. Grianan, one of these, takes its name from a type of temple where the ancient Irish worshipped the sun.

STOP 6

Note the little roads leading inland from the coast. These were formerly the avenues of larger houses now vanished. At the left hand corner of Ballygihan Avenue is the former family house of an Irish writer perhaps noted more in England than Ireland, P-P-Patrick Cambell. His mother, also a writer, was Lady Beatrice Glenavy.

STOP 7

A rather miserable looking little tree here was planted to celebrate the centenary of James Joyce's birth. This now is actually the second tree planted. The first was removed by persons unknown, whether vandals or literary critics, no-one knows. Proceed now through the vaguely sinister little park. On the left through the bushes is the red brick of the former Sandycove Baths. These Victorian sea baths lasted up to about 25 years ago, now a store for a Scuba diving club.

STOP 8

Nice view.

STOP 9

The harbour was built early in the last century to ship granite to Dublin. Note fine stonework of the slipway and, on the road surface at the top, a large iron ring used to haul boats up. The harbour is now silted up and used as a popular beach.

STOP 10

The 'Gentlemans Bathing Place' as signposted is widely known as the Forty Foot, after a British regiment formerly stationed in the adjoining battery. The military abandoned here in 1900 and since then the only battles have been between women and men over the use of the Forty-Foot.Nowadays women who enter are generally given the cold shoulder, and sometimes other parts of the anatomy too, by the men-only diehards.

STOP 11

The Martello Tower, built as a defence against Napoleon, is now a Joycean Museum, the world-renowed novelist James Joyce set the opening of his novel Ulysses here. The museum contains the writer's walking stick and other important literary artefacts. Afterwards proceed up Sandycove Avenue East and at the top we meet the main road. Turn right here.

STOP 12

Just after the traffic lights on our left is the birthplace of Roger Casement rebel hanged a long time ago. Dublin's military airport at Baldonnel takes its name from him but around here he has little memorial, perhaps because of the suspicion that he was homosexual, perhaps because Sandycove is not natural rebel territory.

STOP 13

'Tara Hall' was home of Monk Gibbon, one of those writers that few have ever read but who, through sheer longevity and persistence, establish some form of recognition. A wise and erudite man, by all accounts, but for the twist of fate we would be going to look at his walking stick rather than that of James Joyce.

Sandycove Walk continued on following page >

STOP 14

Queen Victoria's husband is commemorated by the name of Albert Road, here on our left past the pub. Just before Albert Road, interestingly, at the base of the wall by the huge Eucalyptus Globulus trees, was carved in the stone the mysterious initials VMC MM. (But is now gone I see, as I revise this guide!) After all this excitement proceed down the curving hill ahead into Glasthule.

STOP 15

Now positively trendy, Glasthule is a very old settlement, said to take its name from the Irish-language meaning 'Toole's Stream'. Incorrectly said...it takes its name from Irish meaning 'Stream of The Black Foreigners'. This stream still runs underground through the village and into the sea at a place called Bug Rock. An interesting village, there is a strange juxtaposition of some very expensive shops and some rather poor people. Oh weary world!

STOP 16

Apart from the modern alterations, St Josephs Church (Roman Catholic) is a most elegant and peaceful spot to rest from the weariness of the world, to contemplate injustice, and to resolve to improve things as soon as possible.

And that's about enough walking for one day!

Conan Kennedy, your DunLaoghaire guide, is writer of several books on early Ireland, folklore and mythology.

---

*A pull-out map
of DunLaoghaire
and the surrounding area
is on the following page.*